Acts of Light

Acts of Light

—poems by—
Mark Frutkin

Cormorant Books

Published with the assistance of the Canada Council and
the Ontario Arts Council.

Acknowledgments: Nine poems from "Spontaneous
Combustion" first appeared in *Descant*; "The Watering
Hole" series first appeared in *ARC*.

Special thanks to Don McKay and Christopher Dewdney
for editorial suggestions.

Cover from an ink and gouache on card, *End of a dream*,
by Jack Akroyd, courtesy of the artist and the Canada
Council Art Bank.

Printed and bound in Canada.

Published by   Cormorant Books
                  RR 1
                  Dunvegan, Ontario
                  K0C 1J0

Canadian Cataloguing in Publication Data

Frutkin, Mark, 1948-

Acts of light

ISBN 0-920953-70-0

I. Title.

PS8561.R84A73 1992   C811'.54   C92-090028-3
PR9199.3.F78A65 1992

This book is dedicated to my son, Elliot.

ACTS OF LIGHT

CONTENTS

THE WATERING HOLE

Silence

Rimbaud in a sweat
Hesitates over the page
While the earth spins
Thoughts in his head
A kind of steamy weather

Beads of sweat,
Pale moons about to drop
On the blank sheet

All of night has flowed
Through his pen,
Stars over Africa
Fall into themselves

His head fills with jungle chatter
He forgets to breathe,
The empty page
Turning to a ghost
Dissolves in his forehead.

White Sea

Rimbaud swims in a white sea,
The positions of his body,
Flailings of pictographic characters,
Jungle left far behind
Chattering its strange marmalade of sounds.
At the savannah's edge
Yawns the silhouette of a lion.
A bird passes through the perfect
Circle of a snake.
Rimbaud falls asleep
Floating on his back in the sea,
Curled like a fetal moon.
The jungle plays on the surface
Of his skin
Like a film, his nervous system
Turned inside out.

Legend

Rimbaud's white brain
A crumpled map of Africa.
Anything could happen there,
Nothing ever does.
A hippo rolls over in warm
Mud and falls asleep.
Starlight slants into the jungle
Where his eyelids flicker
And night solitaires emit screeches
Heard only in dreams.
Rimbaud a diamond gone to seed,
A vague cirrus
Forgetting its shape.
As his voice fades,
The jungle sprouts new names.

White Moon

Rimbaud and his lost country,
An elephant with the Eiffel
Tower on its back.
He can't see any of this.
His sky blue-black
And cross-hatched with bats at dusk.
He's falling backwards into an over-ripe fruit.
He's a white moon speckled with seed,
A high white flower
Tumbling down the slender throat
Of a giraffe.

Orgasm

Gazelles,
Organs strung together with blue veins
Crowd across the savannah.
Leopards gather at dusk
To darken the earth.
An indigo bird rides
The back of a rhino,
White horn piercing the air.
Rimbaud recalls the sound
Of orgasm but it is no
Sound at all

The Watering Hole

Rimbaud is a white
Sky reflected in the watering hole.
All the beasts have come
And fallen into it.
For a while they continued
As words but the words fade.
Now they are a blank
Page with a strange thirst.

AFRICAN CLOTH

Red Sky Yellow Earth

   Page never quite pure
white, always a shadow
clouds the corner,
a speck of dirt
reflects the light, resists
the void
*

   And from that
speck of dust
sprout jungles, tangles
of longing and release, strange
beetles wrapped in leaves,
eggs with entire unborn
worlds inside, contorted
winds that turn in
upon themselves
*

   A kind of script
consumes the sky.

*
Green winds,
succulent foliage,
carnival of animal
song, a long brown mottled snake
shining and iridescent, a tribe
of cocoa men clicking
like stones in a river——all
of these and more, clouds
coming up over the horizon.

*

African mother
   stone bud
   blossoming dust
*

Listen —
you can hear her cities
crumbling, sand
gathering again
*

African mother
   stone blossom
and deep beneath the surface
   of the earth
a well of tears.

*

A storyteller
casts his spell
  on a gathering
        of slim, listening boys
*

He tells the tale over and over again
  until they remember it
  until they grow old
  and can tell it
                on their own
*

The river nearby
              has never stopped
          running
If it did
      the tale
      would dry up
there would be nothing
left in those fields
        but a tree
        unable to capture the light
        in its fruit.

*

A flower
       splits a rock
*

The earth goes spinning
   in two directions
*

The flower learns
   to sing its own name
   in colour
*

Africa, the song
      of the jungle rising
      in its throat.

*

The entire story
         of red sky
         yellow earth
                 told
in a piece of singing cloth,
the beginning
                                 the end
and what rose and fell between them
*

In the center of the cloth
             the sun
     meets the river,
where African woman
wraps the cloth
             round her thighs.

*

In that land there is nothing

                      to grasp,

tangled green

             flames

   of the river
*

A green parrot passes
a green parrot passes
gone forever
*

In that land there is nothing

                     to grasp

     so you invent
tales to tell

           about the fire

*

the words in the fire
*

the gods in the fire
*

and the silence.

*

Up from white earth stretch
slim silver leaves of steel,
        a red bird like a drop of blood
*

The moon a disturbed
and molten pearl
        dreams backwards
        and forgets,
            slowly paring down the world.

Ode To Africa

O mother of breath
mother of breath
mother of breath
original vowel breathing
while the stick-man
skeleton painted black
drums rain in your dust
his consonants clicking
and now a scarlet lover
he grasps your waist
keeps you bound and turning

Move indolent wind
rousing dust
dance in dream figures
dance in patterns of scarred face
etched breast
and ululate slow brown river
ululate rain and voice

Africa
with your dry tree
and jungle sweating
with your bone and flesh
skull and skin
with your white oxen ploughing

black earth
with your distant mists
exuding silence
and your animals cackling
braying   crying

Follow the jet line of the cheetah
as it threads its life
through a gazelle's heart
the arc of the leopard's neck
as it severs
the young boar's cry

Regard the zebra
caught in the bars
of life and death
the white jaw
of the lion's skull
its roar turned thunder
its blood turned rain

Africa
mother of breath
earth of the first word
first fire   first spear
first magic drum
first hut   circle of huts
drumming village to village
chains of carbon
coming out of itself
charcoal in the fire
black stitches etched on face
back of hand

Squatting in dust
barefoot spinner
threads the cloth
of human life
grinds plants into greens and reds
that radiate dusk and dawn
repeats the patterned endocarp
for thousands of days
eats from the heart
of a wooden bowl

SPONTANEOUS COMBUSTION

Roughly speaking, wrens' songs improve in
direct ratio with the humidity and darkness of
their haunts.
                    —Fuertes

Heart is your only security.
                    —Chogyam Trungpa, *Rinpoche*

Untouchable Heat

New entry
Spontaneous combustion
There are human beings who
For no reason
Burst into flames

And siddhas* who
At will
Can drive their bodies
To emanate untouchable heat

April light.

* Siddhas—Indian and Tibetan holy men with magical powers

Sounds

Language combusts
Spontaneously out of darkness
Smoke over the charnel ground
A ghost of storms
The kind of laugh
One would expect
From Kafka

Neither slave nor master   language
Equal   white   innocent flower
A necklace of skulls   planets
Spinning tops
Each emitting a different sound.

Phosphor Ghost

Indelicate consummation
The fire in 1900
That burned down two-thirds
Of the city of Hull
Swept across the Chaudière Bridge
        (Hyphen)
To cut a mile-wide swath
Through the city of Ottawa

As if the dry page of old ways
Was touched by live wires
At the turn of a century
From far north
A phosphor ghost
Combusted on contact
With the city's frenzied energy

The bridge a triangulation of flame
See the glitter in a horse's eye
See the bridge in the river
One city reflecting another
        (Burn words)

Photographic Verbs

Skeleton of flame and dancing bone
Etches chemical dark
Negative scarred
Scarecrow of light

Photographs of the Fire:
Brilliant tanager verbs writ
Breathless.

Graph

Ecstasy vision trance
Experiment with flint and steel
Spark and twitch
Immolation goldfish catching light

A calendar of planets
Numbers plotting spring

Dancing sticks conjure heat
Invent words   glossolalia
Speak in tongues
Ardent fish
Gold-speckled river
Jangle of bracelets
All along alarm.

Gilgamesh

Golden lions play in moonlight
Mating animated flames
Shadows of brass horses
Like a child's toy
Turn against the wall

A sunflower
Dressed in a glowing mane
Turns and returns
Tournesol / carouse / carousel

Ignition / dawn / text
Moon a mouth shouting Sun!

Text

Graph of flame along a flood-mark
When golden fish swam attics
And sun
Set with a splash

Walls of Uruk
Ghosted into ash

Paraphs of albacore
Texts of cuneiform flood
Arsoned.

Etymon

No past or future to speak of
All lost
But this etymon
This moment of grief or hunger
No vocabulary for disaster
Mute but alive

Baptism by fire
Styles of language
Apocalypse or liberation
Learn the lexicon of songbird.

Skeleton Song

Siddhas burn til exhausted
Nothing left but ictal ash ictal ghost
Cleansed by fire and water
Words worked
Down to bone

Turns   turns himself and turns
To rain and rain and sun and sun
Relic of ritual song
A skeleton tree
To drape green light.

Flint On Heart

Minor spark
Flint on heart
Stormy conflagrations
Of madness or liberation

Single note instigates flood
One stone removed
Topples city walls

Light arcs across
Heaven's synapse
Moist air   charged earth
Wingbeat brainstorm.

Red-winged

Tree's green stutter
Eurhythmic drumbeat
Arithmetic pulse

Windows explode
In the heat of song

Red-winged
Blackbird robin cardinal
Geometries of thalamus cloud
Flood starts from the inner chambers
Of the heart
The mouth storms
The brain bursts into flame
Words released and ghosted
From the body of the norm.

ACTS OF LIGHT

"but already I could feel my being turned —
instinct and intellect balanced equally
as in a wheel whose motion nothing jars —
by the Love that moves the Sun and the other
stars."

—from *The Paradiso*, Canto XXXIII,
lines 143-146. Translation by John Ciardi.

I

Radiant

At 35 years of age Dante
Wandered through a forest of spiralling trees,
Came to a pool
Reflecting a potent void
Where his imagination leapt   a star
Shooting down the spine
Of the Milky Way

On its surface it was 1300
Will always be 1300
As Dante gazed down into the heavens
Where the sun makes its dangerous
Journey through darkness
Where the fish are radiant
And everyone remembers the future.

Boustrophedon

Night
A black night in spring
Dante slept under the leaking dugs of the stars

He dreamt a half-read book in an empty room
A book written in boustrophedon
Right to left then
Left to right

We don't know which half
Was read first
As Dante dreamt
Of an ox-head turning
At the end of a furrow.

All Weathers At Once

It rained   the sun shone
Huge white clouds folded into themselves
The stars   Blackest night
All weathers at once
The world a woman
Giving birth to a girl child
Over and over again.

II

Earthquake

Long ago an earthquake drove the crows from the willows
Rent Dante's brain in two
And words poured out

Dante consulted an oracle who perched in a tree
Listening to the wind in leaves
And brass plates chiming like lucent fruit

She could see distant armies
Breaching the walls of the city
Dark clouds marching on the horizon

Dante's head ached as he watched
The oracle turn hermaphroditic

He told her his brain had been split in half
That he was obsessed with numbers
That a certain star came to him in dreams
Stared at him through the window

In between Heaven and Earth   she said
Is nothing but motion

Mercurial space   the source
Of wind bees spring and music
Stay between   she said
Stay in the fever.

Invoking the Name of Hermes

Dante remembered she had invoked the name
Of Hermes who is silver   who moves like mercury
When she became his lover in the city of Corinth

He anointed her sex with sap from a rootless tree
And the split in the trunk of her form
Echoed the split in his brain
The memory of forked lightning   earth opening
Descriptions of the world pour out.

Prophecy

When the earthquake struck it awoke
All the bells in the swaying church towers

The tongue of a snake forked down from heaven
In that flash everyone was conceived

Like speech   a rain of light fell
As Dante ate the middle page of the oracle's book
Acquiring the power
At some point in the future
To prophesy the past.

III

Script

In the early spring branch of the willow
Dante noticed the Aramaic "shin"
Or was it the "kaf"
Waxy fists of buds unfolding
A forest of undeciphered script

Light itself is cursive   he mused
Trees spiral out and spiral in
Brilliant at the edge
Where sun curls along a stem

And the wind
The same wind that shook speech
Loose from the tangle of oracle hair
Spun a mask that hung from a branch
Sap dripping from its tongue

Its gaze fructified fields
Edged by a river
In the shape of an S.

Horsehead Nebula

The ox bellowed and the world caught fire
While Dante floated in the orchid boat
With his lover   the oracle

In a nearby field an apiarist
Set fire to old hives
The oracle washed her breasts
While Dante dreamt the Horsehead nebula
At that moment   a horse caught fire
On the streets of Hiroshima

The ox bellowed again
The energy of bees filled the air
Cicadas etched in the long heat
In a southern village a hyena
Was set on fire for a festival
The villagers imitated its shriek
A fish burst screaming from the water
Flew toward the sun

The ox bellowed again
Standing in a grove of olive trees
Bellowed out his pain again   again

The oracle turned and quieted Dante's
Mouth with her own.

The Drum Gives Way to the Flute

Dante examined monumental script
On stele of granite
In Phoenicia in Sumeria in Akkadia
In Egypt Greece Italy

He slept in stalls with oxen
Near villages where tribes had stopped
And stood thousands of years before
Piling stone upon stone
When they stopped they noticed the stars
Kept turning

Orion the nomadic hunter
Gave way to Boötes the Plowman
All this reflected in the river
As the drum gave way to the flute

The newborn shook his rattle
Like the tail of a snake
Stone lingams stood tall
Folded back the dark
And private parts of a cloud.

IV

Names

Fish / ox head / serpent / sign / praying figure
This was another of Dante's names
Dal alp nun ta he

Looking into himself
He found that his name kept changing
With each gull that passed with each
Sound of ox grunt or groan or sigh
Of woman or child with each ripple
Of water pulsing like a swollen vein
His name changed and he was beginning
To grow familiar with each word
That pulsed through his mind and recognize
Each as his own and not his own
He was for the first time   still alone.

Melting

Lines of dawn
Drawn in a pool
Winter constellations gave way to those of spring
Orion's bow retired on the wall
Appeared in books as the letter S
Boötes' plow hung over the shoulders of the ox
A wooden frame shaped like an A

It was the time of doubling forms
The invention of mirrors and phenomenal illusions
Liquid fire charged and echoing
In the eyes of lovers.

Vernal Equinox

Twelve hours of light   twelve of dark
The ox high above the equator turned his head
A new furrow to plow

Twelve hours on the clock
A kite of bees in the shape of an ox
Led on by a small girl with a light
Held aloft in her palms

She was the oracle with the rose in her thighs
Offering the future to gods
Casting the past to beasts
But Dante remained human
Unfolding her sex into cities

And stars fell like snow
On half the world
At noon and midnight
Sighs and ecstatic cries form another language.

V

Deep Space

The three stars of Orion's belt Dante named
The String of Pearls
The source of his dream
A dream in the middle of night
In the middle of his life

Swirling out of deep space
Dante a fish in a spiral galaxy
Falling to earth from his mother's loins
A reed boat took him through the land
Of Akkadia on a river coiling like a serpent
Full of silver stars and milk and ghosts

In a city shaped like a rose
He wandered for years in the dark
Wielding a silver scalpel
Incising a precise
Line in a heart he knew was his own.

Rain

Dante sang a hundred songs on the hills above Firenze
Music emanating from the earth entered him
Through the perineum rising along the spine
And spilling into the wind
Opalescent resin from a rootless tree

The same wind that shook light loose
From leaves shimmering with oracle speech
Took the ice from the river
And melted the stars.

Shroud

To hasten winter's death
The oracle spoke of the black shroud
She was sewing for Dante
And how she would throw it
In a pool of sunset
When the water was in flames

The shroud sank like a shadow out of sight
As stars began to appear in the sky

And then she was silent

To speak of it was enough
To voice the idea enough
There was no shroud   no dark pool
No oracle   no stars   no Dante
But there was an intricate tale
That learned how to repeat itself
In the mind of the future
A jewel of light
That appeared and vanished
In each moment   never quite the same.

VI

Burning Horse

The energy of stars
Mingled and split
On entering her jewel of salt-
Water flame

A storm of love
Inside a burning horse.

VII

Zero(( ))Font

Heaven never tired of its zero dream
Rose of the split in the rock
Rose of the empty sky

Love stormed inside a burning horse
Groundzero((((((( ))))))fontanelle
And the fetus turns its head   listening

This is the naming of names
A grid of light
Placed over acts of light.

VIII

Drum

The belly of the oracle stretches and swells
As she murmurs the names
Of wind and leaf and light
The names of star and fish
Whispers the names of fire that end in ash
All the names of bird and fruit
And dust and seed
And water that always
Ends in ocean and sounds like river
The names of colour and music
The names of tree root and rose and city
And time and ice and army and atom
And myth and god and beast and human
And the fetus turns its head   listening.

IX

Lemons

As she picks lemons
That sway in the breeze
Dante remembers when he was thirteen
They had gelded the ox and given the testes to him
And now she comes rippling with song
Her basket overflowing
With bitter light.

Scapula Wings

Wings for the child   she says
Removing a pair of scapula
From the ashes of a fire

We are half-way there   she says
Gazing at markings on the bones
Throwing one as far as she can south
Shouting   The past is not fixed
And the other flying north
As she shouts   The future remains open

The bees of spring are half-awake   half-mad
Easing their frenzy in the fire of flowers

Clouds form a hieratic frieze of script
At the horizon edge of sky
Her body cursive as a willow.

Mimetic Ritual

The city grows like salt   crystal   diamond
In the distance the oracle ebbs into a flute

Through the power of sympathetic magic
The head of a drum   a calm sea   tremble

In a mimetic ritual of deep space
Dante meditates on a pure and dimensionless number
While slow stars appear
Throwing out glistening spars of light.

X

Layers

Layers of city ancient and repetitive
Duality doubled   duality's square
Illusion of time and structure
Echo / empathy / mimesis / mirror / rhyme / water

The heat of her loins
Ripened by belief in the sun

The stars of her organs   stars
Within those and the stars within those.

A Sympathy of Forms

Music of prophets with long memories
Entices her body out of spring
Desires the weaving of planets and stars
Conjunctions of stone and cloud
Prime numbers dividing into themselves

The lingam a stone flute
The subtle split in its crown
Where lips fold back and music pours out
Emanates a form of sympathy / a sympathy of forms
Resonates with the speaking wind
Magnetizes poles into perfect spinning.

The Size of Paper

Her olive body painted with white rings
The oracle dances in a circle of drums
White ring at her feet
White circle at the top of her head

As the drums speak to her she speaks to the heavens
As stars find the dark of her waters
And shift there in pure brilliant systems
She drives through the stem and root of earth

Translations of chaos   forests of script
City of pure form   rose of no meaning

Dante holds a paper the size of the human head

A flute of flesh scored with moist openings
She magnetizes vast and minute musics.

XI

Furrow

Dante plays Prometheus Forethought
Bound to the sun
Drowning in the sea glistening along her thighs
An ox lowing in the rain
As he turns another furrow of verse
In the willing androgynous earth.

Surface

Cannot be described but includes words

Music music   the oracle would turn to dust
The garrulous tree of streams dry up
Exhaust itself   Wait hopelessly for rain
Even of this he would sing

Red and blue deserts and desert skies
All weathers at once

The surface of the water
Remains still and potent
Immaculate number / immortal space.

Mining the Heavens

Sound of machines in the distance
Salt / silver / iron / gold
Eighty-eight days for Mercury to round the sun
Number of music doubled
The eloquent guide
Messenger close to the sun's side

That which was brought out of the deep
Dark of mines shines in the light
Bright steel gear at the center of Copernican dreams

The oracle spins in a radiant spring wind
Cities vector across the plains.

XII

Net of Light

The tree a net of light
Casts itself up into stars

Dante an old calligrapher
Dips his brush in the river
Watches the passing of beauty

As he draws the character for "lake" with black ink
Silver nebulae drift in the sky
Drawing the character for "wind"
The particles of the oracle
Come dancing to him.

Cloud of Bees

The oracle smiles a lover's smile
Parentheses radiating from the corners of her mouth

The dawn of tragedy
The first morning of the Great Dyonesia
In Athens at the end of March

Her face and his
Volatile as masks
Two characters trading voice
And expression across time

Old hives in the distance burn
A cloud of bees swirls like lovers
Above fields of spring

Their faces flicker through the seasons
An alphabet of images glances from the water
Dante leans forward and kisses
The still heart of the lake.

The Plow of the Ox Unearths

The plow of the ox unearths a bell
A new planet   a clock
A season shining with rain
A mycellium that hangs among the stars
Like a pulsating net
Nebula   cloud   breath

The plow of the ox unearths
A storm of dreams
Caught on a primal stone

The plow of the ox unearths
The decaying grave of Einstein
A black spider with a sack of white eggs on her back
A mask that fell from a tree

Dante bids the beast turn at the end of the furrow
For this field is written in boustrophedon.

XIII

Ancient Patterns

A young girl   the sea   kisses
Her old lover then scurries away
Teasing the life out of him

Dante is Odysseus on her now
Riding a siren's song
The night a fruit bright with seed

Constellations of shining fish
Follow the ancient patterns
While inventing the future

The ship cuts like an ox and plow
Dante swimming in the oracle body

The moon high above swells with light.

Fault Line

A moment before the beginning
A fatigue in the pattern
A fault line reaching down into primal
Depths and climbing the heavens

An old hunter rich with tales
Orion passes quietly from this life
While Boötes ploughs up spring

Dante mixes his speech
With that of the oracle
The walls of the city begin to crumble
Music shifts the stars
As new nebulae like stormy nets
Break over the sea.

The Chinese Character For "Man"

Half-way through his allotted time
Of three score years and ten
Dante mounts the long stairs
To the window where a single star
Wanes in the dawn

The oracle is with him
Yet he remains alone

A star drifts down from deep space
Turns like an owl
Swirls like a leaf

A trout in its veils
Spirals up from the timeless deep

The old calligrapher brushes the Chinese
Character for "man"
In the wind
Across the heavens
On the surface of the water
In every leaf of a tree at Delphi
In the breath of Dante
And in the breath of the oracle
Draws it in the light of day
And in the vanishing dark
Draws it on the head of the child
As the child breaks the surface
And all things are born.

NOTES
Acts of Light

Radiant / Page 47
The Divine Comedy begins with Dante's descent into the Inferno before dawn on Good Friday in the year 1300. He was thirty-five years old, half the "three score years and ten" allotted to a lifetime by the Bible.
(In Dante's *Inferno*) "there is little that is peculiarly Christian . . . It is not a theological arrangement but a philosophical one." (John Ciardi, Introduction to *The Purgatorio*, Mentor, 1957)

Boustrophedon / Page 48
"Boustrophedon" — From Greek "bous", ox, and "strephein", to turn. "Furrow" — Akin to the Rumanian "versta", a line or row and the Middle Latin "versus", a furrow or a turning. Also, a line of verse.

Invoking the Name of Hermes / Page 51
"A rootless tree" — Zen Buddhist term for one who has attained liberation.

Prophecy / Page 52
"All the bells in the swaying church towers" — From an eyewitness account of the 1906 San Francisco earthquake in which the tolling of bells preceded the collapse of churches and other buildings.

Script / Page 53
"The Aramaic 'shin'" — The ancestor of the letter "S" which appeared about 1500 B.C. as the Proto-Canaanite or Proto-Sinaitic pictograph of a bow.
"Kaf" — Hebrew and Arabic source for the letter "K", from a Proto-Canaanite pictograph of the palm of the hand.
"A mask that hangs from a branch" — A Greek tradition for ensuring fertility in the fields.

Horsehead Nebula / Page 54
"The orchid boat" — An ancient Chinese poetic term for vagina.

Names / Page 56
"Fish" — Pictographic source for the letter "D" (Arabic "dal").
"Ox head" — Pictographic source for the letter "A" (Canaanite "alp", Hebrew "aluf").
"Serpent" — Pictographic source for the letter "N" (Hebrew and Arabic "nun").
"Sign" — Pictographic source for the letter "T" (Arabic "ta").
"Praying figure" — Pictographic source for the letter "E" (Hebrew "he").
"Dal alp nun ta he" — DANTE (Source: *Origins of the Alphabet* by Joseph Naveh. Cassell, London, 1975.)

Vernal Equinox / Page 58
"Led on by a small girl" — Inspired by one of Picasso's Minotaur etchings.

Zero(( ))Font / Page 63
"Groundzero((((((( ))))))fontanelle" — The middle line of the middle poem. It contains 33 units to echo the 33 poems of the whole. The center unit is an empty space. The line brings together two seeming extremes of energy: the central point of a nuclear explosion and the boneless area at the top of a baby's skull. The top of the skull is also believed to be the general area from which the liberated spirit exits the body.

Drum / Page 64
"And the fetus turns its head listening" — In traditional Inuit culture, during labour the grandmother would chant names at random. It was believed the child would make its appearance when it heard its own name called.

Scapula Wings / Page 66
"A pair of scapula" — Flat, triangular shoulder blade bones found in man and other vertebrates. Burned and then read for divinatory revelations by the ancient Chinese.

A Sympathy of Forms / Page 69
"The lingam a stone flute" — "The lingam (literally 'symbol') is often taken as a phallic symbol but is actually the integration of the masculine and the feminine. In China, the lingam is called 'Kuei'; it is an oblong piece of jade terminating in a triangle. The seven stars of the Great Bear are often engraved on the Kuei. . ." (J.E. Cirlot, *A Dictionary of Symbols*).

Cloud of Bees / Page 75
"The Great Dyonesia" — An important spring festival held in ancient Athens, in which theatrical tragedies competed with each other.
"Volatile as masks" — In ancient Greece it was common for a single actor to play a number of roles, both male and female, while narrating the tales of Homer.

The Chinese Character For "Man" / Page 79
At the end of the Inferno, Dante and his guide, Virgil, exit from the lower regions just before dawn on Easter Sunday.

The question of form was essential to Dante. The Divine Comedy was constructed of one hundred cantos in this way: 1-33-33-33. Changes in perception demand changes in form. *Acts of Light* speaks of the world radiating forth from the fountain of emptiness at the centre of which is man attempting to harmonize heaven and earth.